W9-BFB-739

DISCARD

OLD ADOBE
SCHOOL LIBRARY

796.2
Rad   Radlauer, Dan   c.1
                                Ado
        Skateboard mania

		DATE DUE	

796.2
Rad.   Radlauer, Dan   c.1
                                Ado
        Skateboard mania

Skateboard Mania

By The Radlauers
Dan, Robin, and Ed

AN ELK GROVE BOOK

 CHILDRENS PRESS, CHICAGO

Created by Radlauer Productions, Inc. for Childrens Press

The authors thank BAHNE-CADILLAC for their
cooperation during skateboard competition photography.

Library of Congress Cataloging in Publication Data

Radlauer, Dan.
    Skateboard mania.

    (Ready, get set, go)
    ''An Elk Grove book.''
    SUMMARY: Simple text and photographs introduce the
techniques of riding a skateboard.
    1. Skateboards—Juvenile literature. [1. Skateboards]
I. Radlauer, Robin, joint author. II. Radlauer, Edward,
joint author. III. Title.
GV851.R32   796.2'1   75-23460
ISBN 0-516-07411-3

Copyright © 1976 by Regensteiner Publishing Enterprises, Inc.
All rights reserved. Published simultaneously in Canada.
Printed in the United States of America

    3 4 5 6 7 8 9 10 11 12 13 14 15 R 82 81 80 79 78 77

Ready, Get Set, Go Books

Ready

Motorcycle Mania
Flying Mania
Skateboard Mania

Get Set

Fast, Faster, Fastest
Wild Wheels
Racing Numbers

Go

Soap Box Racing
Ready, Get Set, Whoa!
Model Airplanes

Skateboard mania?

Yes, it's skateboard mania.

Wheels?

A skateboard has four small wheels.

Board?

The board is where you put your feet.

Tricks?

If you're a good skateboard rider,
you can do good tricks.

Handstand?

**A handstand takes strong hands
and strong arms.**

Wheelie?

This is a good way to do a wheelie.

Wheelie?

You can even do a backward wheelie.

Skill and balance?

**You need skill and balance
to ride a surfboard.**

Skill and balance?

**Racing down a skateboard ramp
takes skill, balance, and steering, too.**

Steering?

**To steer to the right, lean to the right.
To steer to the left, lean to the left.**

Fast?

If you're going this fast, be careful.

Slow?

**If you're not very careful,
you might go very slow.**

Fun?

Skateboards are fun.
Riding with friends is even more fun.

Skateboard mania?

Yes, it's skateboard mania.

OLD ADOBE
SCHOOL LIBRARY